This Book Belongs To

_____

_____

VISIT OUR AUTHOR PAGE
at
AMAZON

Scan This

Copyright © Pixelart studio

COLOR TEST

NOTICE!

★ All you need is a pencil, eraser and color.

★ It's not necessary to pick real life color, pick whatever color you like most. You can even mix colors!

★ Draw lightly at first. Add details according to the diagrams, but don't worry about being perfect!

★ Sometimes colors appear differently than you expect. The color test page is a great way to try out colors and shading beforehand.

★ Start on an image whatever you feel comfortable. There's no wrong place to begin! Don't worry if your drawings don't turn out the way you want to. Just take a break, come to it later. Sometimes drawing the same thing for a few times will help.

NOW LET'S COLOR!

Color This Page

Color This Page

Color This Page

Color This Page

Color This Page

Color This Page

Color This Page

Color This Page

Color This Page

Color This Page

Color This Page

Color This Page

Color This Page

Color This Page

Color This Page

Color This Page

Color This Page

Color This Page

Color This Page

Color This Page

Color This Page

Color This Page

Color This Page

Color This Page

Color This Page

Color This Page

Color This Page

Color This Page

Color This Page

Color This Page

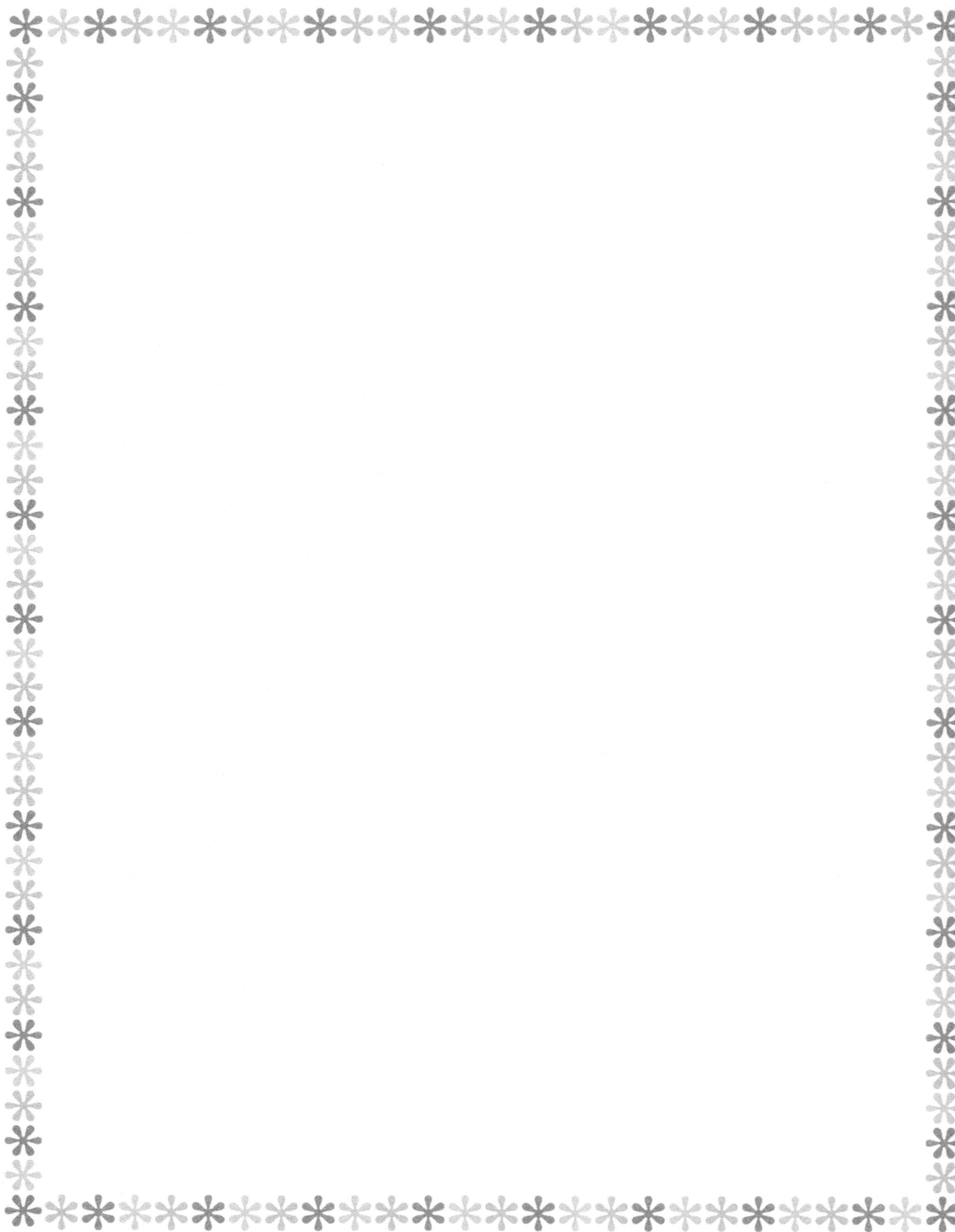

HEY!
WE WOULD LOVE
TO HEAR FROM YOU.

PLEASE LEAVE "*PIXELART STUDIO*" A REVIEW. YOUR FEEDBACKS AND OPINION CAN HELP US TO CREAT BETTER PRODUCTS FOR YOU.

COLORING BOOK..

Thank You!

Made in the USA
Las Vegas, NV
22 August 2021